D0461706

SUPER
SANDCASTLE
Poetry Power

FIREWORKS
~ TO ~
FRUITCAKE

Reading, Writing, and Reciting
Poems About Holidays

COMPILED & EDITED BY SUSAN M. FREESE   ILLUSTRATED BY JAN WESTBERG

ABDO
Publishing Company

Published by ABDO Publishing Company, 8000 West 78th Street, Edina, MN 55439. Copyright © 2008 by Abdo Consulting Group, Inc. International copyrights reserved in all countries. No part of this book may be reproduced in any form without written permission from the publisher. Super SandCastle™ is a trademark and logo of ABDO Publishing Company.

Printed in the United States.

Editor: Pam Price
Curriculum Coordinator: Nancy Tuminelly
Cover and Interior Design and Production: Mighty Media

Library of Congress Cataloging-in-Publication Data

Freese, Susan M., 1958-
  Fireworks to fruitcake : reading, writing, and reciting poems about holidays / Susan M. Freese.
    p. cm. -- (Poetry power)
  Includes index.
  ISBN 978-1-60453-004-9
  1. Poetry--Authorship--Juvenile literature. 2. Children's poetry, American. 3. Holidays in literature--Juvenile literature. I. Title.

PN1059.A9F744 2008
808.1--dc22

2007038977

Super SandCastle™ books are created by a team of professional educators, reading specialists, and content developers around five essential components— phonemic awareness, phonics, vocabulary, text comprehension, and fluency— to assist young readers as they develop reading skills and strategies and increase their general knowledge. All books are written, reviewed, and leveled for guided reading, early intervention reading, and Accelerated Reader® programs for use in shared, guided, and independent reading and writing activities to support a balanced approach to literacy instruction.

About SUPER SANDCASTLE™

Bigger Books for Emerging Readers
Grades PreK–3

Created for library, classroom, and at-home use, Super SandCastle™ books support and engage young readers as they develop and build literacy skills and will increase their general knowledge about the world around them. Super SandCastle™ books are part of SandCastle™, the leading preK–3 imprint for emerging and beginning readers. Super SandCastle™ features a larger trim size for more reading fun.

Let Us Know

Super SandCastle™ would like to hear your stories about reading this book. What was your favorite page? Was there something hard that you needed help with? Share the ups and downs of learning to read. We want to hear from you! Send us an e-mail.
sandcastle@abdopublishing.com

Contact us for a complete list of SandCastle™, Super SandCastle™, and other nonfiction and fiction titles from ABDO Publishing Company.
www.abdopublishing.com
8000 West 78th Street Edina, MN 55439
800-800-1312 · 952-831-1632 fax

A Note to Librarians, Teachers, and Parents

The poems in this book are grouped into three sections. "I Can Read" has poems that children can read on their own. "Read With Me" has poems that may require some reading help. "Kids' Corner" has poems written by children.

There are some words in these poems that young readers may not know. Some of these words are in boldface. Their pronunciations and definitions are given in the text. Other words can be looked up in the book's glossary.

When possible, children should first read each poem out loud. That way they will hear all of the sounds and feel all of the rhythms. If it is not possible to read aloud, instruct them to read the poems to themselves so they hear the words in their heads.

The **Poetry Pal** next to each poem explains how the poet uses words and specific styles or techniques to make the reader feel or know something.

The **Speak Up!** sidebar prompts readers to reflect on what they think each poem means and how it relates to them.

Become a Poet! provides ideas and activities to encourage and enhance learning about reading, writing, and reciting poetry.

Contents

What is

Let's pretend someone has asked you to write about your favorite holiday. Maybe that is Halloween or Christmas. But you have to follow these rules for writing. First, you can't use very many words. And second, you have to put the words in order so they make a rhyme or a rhythm when you read them.

These are some of the rules for writing poetry. Poetry is different from the writing you do at school and other places, which is called **prose** (PROZE). Here's how!

Poets, the people who write poetry, use fewer words than other kinds of writers. That means they have to pick just the right words to say what they think and feel. The words in poems often are about how things look, feel, smell, taste, and sound. Poets use words to paint pictures for their readers.

taste

sound

smell

feel

look

Dictionary

poetry?

Poets also arrange words in ways to create rhyme and rhythm. You probably know that words that **rhyme** (RIME) sound the same, such as *cat*, *sat*, and *bat*. Rhyming words are fun to say and to hear. A **rhythm** (RIH-thum) is a pattern of sounds. Think about the beat you feel when you clap or march to music. You can feel the same kind of beat when you read a poem. By using rhythm and rhyme, poets make words sound like music.

What else is special about poetry? Because of all the choices poets get to make when they write, no two poems are ever the same. You will see that when you read the poems in this book! And you will find that out when you write your own poems too!

C
S → at
B

Getting Started

The terms on the next page tell how poets choose words and put them together in special ways. As you read about each term, look at the poem "Halloween" to see an example.

Halloween

BY SYDNEY FOSS

Pumpkin faces glowing bright
Light my way this special night.

Door to door I trick or treat
Bringing home good things to eat!

line

A line in a poem is a group of words written across the page. In "Halloween," the first line is "Pumpkin faces glowing bright." Each new line starts below the one before it. There are four lines in this short poem.

stanza
(STAN-zuh)

A stanza is a group of lines in a poem that are usually about the same idea. A stanza is like a paragraph in other kinds of writing. Stanzas are separated by blank lines of space. "Halloween" has two stanzas.

rhyme
(RIME)

Words that rhyme end with the same sound, such as *dog* and *log* and *fox* and *socks*. In a poem, the last words of the lines often rhyme but not always. In many poems, every pair of lines rhymes or every other line rhymes. In "Halloween," lines 1 and 2 rhyme and lines 3 and 4 rhyme. Look for the words *bright* and *night* and *treat* and *eat*.

rhythm
(RIH-thum)

Even poems that don't rhyme have rhythm, a pattern of sounds or beats. In most poems, some sounds are accented. That means you say them with a little more punch. Read "Halloween" aloud and listen to which sounds you accent. Clap on these sounds to help you hear and feel them. You probably read line 1 using a pattern like this, "**PUMP**-kin **FA**-ces **GLOW**-ing **BRIGHT**." To read this line, you accent every other sound, starting with the first one. Line 2 has the same pattern, and so do lines 3 and 4. All the lines in this poem have the same rhythm.

I Can Read

Have fun reading the poems in this section on your own. If you have trouble, just ask someone for help!

Happy Birthday

BY ROBERT POTTLE

Chocolate ice cream up my nose.
Frosting ear to ear.
Feeding candles to the cat.
Party time is here.

Funny hats on all the pets.
Soda on the floor.
Although I'm turning eight today,
I'm acting like I'm four.

10

Wearing of the Green

BY AILEEN FISHER

It ought to come in April,
or, better yet, in May
when everything is green as green—
I mean St. Patrick's Day.

With still a week of winter
this wearing of the green
seems rather out of season—
it's rushing things, I mean.

But maybe March is better
when all is done and said:
St. Patrick brings a promise,
a four-leaf-clover promise,
a green-all-over promise
of springtime just ahead!

POETRY PAL

This poem is unusual because it has stanzas with different numbers of lines. A stanza with four lines is called a **quatrain** (KWA-train). A stanza with six lines is called a **sestet** (ses-TET).

Can you figure out the rhyme scheme? In each stanza, line 2 rhymes with the last line.

SPEAK UP!

St. Patrick's Day is in March, when spring starts. What's your favorite season or month? Why?

Christmas Dinner

BY KENN NESBITT AND LINDA KNAUS

Fruitcake.
Candied yams.
Mincemeat.
Roast hams.
Eggnog.
Turkey legs.
Aspic.
Deviled eggs.
Gravy.
Dinner rolls.
Take some.
Pass the bowls.
Jell-O.
Christmas punch.
Cookies.
Munch, munch, munch.
Stuffing.
Gingerbread.
Whoops, I'm
overfed!
After
such a load,
feel like
I'll explode.
Guess I'm
gonna die,
so please
pass the pie.

12

Halloween Boo

BY Eileen Spinelli

Boo! says the moon.
Boo! says the cat.
Boo! says the owl.
Boo! says the bat.
Boo! says the scarecrow.
Boo! says the mouse.
Boo! says the shadow
in back of the house.
Boo! says the spider.
Boo! says the crow.
Boo! says the broom
on the patio.
Boo! says the wheel
on the rusty old track.

I say
it's time someone
booed them all back.
All together now...

13

POETRY PAL

Count how many lines begin with the same three words, *Boo! says the*. Repeating words in a poem is called **repetition** (rep-uh-TIH-shun).

Poets use repetition to create rhythm. Every time you say the word *Boo!* you probably say it with a little punch. It's like you're really saying boo to someone.

SPEAK UP!

Think of something that scares you. Why is it scary? What would make it less scary?

Poets also use repetition to show important ideas. Repeating *Thank You* at the start of each stanza shows that being thankful is an important idea in this poem.

The rest of the stanza lists things to be thankful for. Stanza 1 lists things to touch and taste. Stanza 2 lists things to see. What kinds of things are listed in stanza 3? Words about touching, seeing, hearing, smelling, and tasting are called **sensory details** (SEN-sore-ee DEE-tales).

Thanksgiving

BY IVY O. EASTWICK

Thank You
  for all my hands can hold—
    apples red,
      and melons gold,
        yellow corn
          both ripe and sweet,
          peas and beans
            so good to eat!

Thank You
  for all my eyes can see—
    lovely sunlight,
      field and tree,
        white cloud-boats
          in a sea-deep sky,
          soaring bird
            and butterfly.

Thank You
  for all my ears can hear—
    birds' song
      echoing
        far and near,
          songs of little
            stream, big sea,
              cricket, bullfrog,
                duck and bee!

SPEAK UP!

As quickly as you can, write down 10 things you are thankful for. Then look over your list and circle the five things you are most thankful for. Why are these things important to you?

moo

Read With Me

neigh

Enjoy reading these poems with someone who can help you with the harder words and ideas. Poetry is more fun when you understand what you are reading!

At the Farm

BY ROBERT POTTLE

I heard a rabbit go, "oink oink."
I heard a duck go, "moo."
I heard a pig out in the mud
go, "cock-a-doodle-doo."

I'm sure I heard the horses quack,
and then the roosters neigh.
"Old MacDonald had a Farm"
was never sung this way.

The sounds these creatures ought to make
are taught in all the schools,
but disregard those lessons learned;
today is April Fool's!

18

Valentine's Day Card

BY KENN NESBITT

I'd rather fight a tiger, covered head-to-toe in gravy.
I'd rather spend a decade scrubbing toilets in the navy.
I'd rather hug a porcupine; I'd rather wrestle eels.
I'd rather run a marathon with splinters in my heels.
I'd rather sleep on mattresses of razorblades and nails.
I'd rather try to skinny-dip with starving killer whales.
I'd rather be tormented by a gang of angry punks.
I'd rather share a bedroom with a family of skunks.
I'd rather dine on Brussels sprouts and spinach for a year.
I'd rather ride a camel race with blisters on my rear.
I'd rather eat a half a ton of liverwurst and lard
than say how much I like you in this Valentine's Day card.

Everything about this poem is silly! The speaker is looking for new reindeer for Santa, because the other ones have gotten old. They are grumpy and have lots of funny problems.

The feeling or mood that a poem creates is called the **tone** (TOHN).

SPEAK UP!

Pretend you are picking new reindeer for Santa. What do you think they should be able to do?

HELP WANTED

BY TIMOTHY TOCHER

Santa needs new reindeer.
The first bunch has grown old.
Dasher has arthritis;
Comet hates the cold.
Prancer's sick of staring
at Dancer's big behind.
Cupid married Blitzen
and Donder lost his mind.
Dancer's mad at Vixen
for stepping on his toes.
Vixen's being thrown out—
she laughed at Rudolph's nose.
If you are a reindeer
we hope you will apply.
There is just one tricky part:
You must know how to fly.

At Easter

BY EILEEN SPINELLI

Daffodils in April light—
bloom bright.

Robin on the garden seat—
sing sweet.

Baby rabbit in your nest—
be blessed.

World with last year's dreams askew—
all is new.

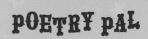

POETRY PAL

The short stanzas of this poem paint pictures with words, creating **imagery** (IM-udge-ree).

As you read, you can probably see in your mind the daffodil, the robin, and the baby rabbit. All of these **images** (IM-uh-juzz) are things that are new in spring, the time of Easter.

SPEAK UP!

Draw or paint a picture of one of the images in this poem.

The Flag Goes By

BY HENRY HOLCOMB BENNETT

Hats off!
Along the street there comes
A blare of bugles, a ruffle of drums,
A flash of color beneath the sky:
Hats off!
The flag is passing by!

Blue and crimson and white it shines,
Over the steel-tipped, ordered lines.
Hats off!
The colors before us fly;
But more than the flag is passing by…

Sign of a nation, great and strong
To ward her people from foreign wrong:
Pride and glory and honor,—all
Live in the colors to stand or fall.

Hats off!
Along the street there comes
A blare of bugles, a ruffle of drums;
And loyal hearts are beating high:
Hats off!
The flag is passing by!

Speak Up!

Most people are proud of where they live. What do you like about where you live? What would you tell other people to make them want to live there?

Light the Festive Candles for Hanukkah

BY AILEEN FISHER

Light the first of eight tonight—
the farthest candle to the right.

Light the first and second, too,
when tomorrow's day is through.

Then light three, and then light four—
every dusk one candle more

Till all eight burn bright and high,
honoring a day gone by

When the Temple was restored,
rescued from the Syrian lord,

And an eight-day feast proclaimed—
The Festival of Lights—well named

To celebrate the joyous day
when we regained the right to pray
to our one God in our own way.

Big Words, Strong Words:
Martin Luther King, Jr.

BY BOBBI KATZ

They called him M.L.
the little boy who rough-housed with his brother
who sat between his mother
and his grandmother on Sunday mornings,
listening to his father's sermons.
He listened more to the rhythm
of the words
than to the words themselves—
words he did not always understand.
He felt the grown-ups around him
carried by the words—
the way the current carried branches
and even trees
down the stream.
He saw the strength of words—their power.
"Someday," he told his mother,
"I'm going to get me some words—
big words, strong words."

And he did.

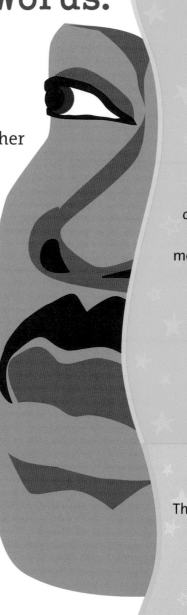

25

POETRY PAL

Martin Luther King Day
is in January. It honors
the life of a man who
wanted everyone to
have the same rights.

This poem about him
doesn't look or sound like
other poems. It sounds
more like someone talking.
This kind of poem is
called **free verse**.

SPEAK UP!

The poem talks a lot about
the power of words.
How can words help
people? How can words
hurt people?

POETRY PAL

A **What Am I?** poem gives readers clues to lead them to the subject. To write this kind of poem, first think of a subject. You can write about a holiday or some part of one. Then write down sensory details about your subject. How does it look, sound, feel, taste, and smell?

Choose the best three sensory details, and write them down as lines 1, 2, and 3 of your poem. Add your subject as line 4.

What Am I?

BY SAREE FOWLER

Flashing in the sky
Red, blue, green, and gold
Popping and crackling
Fireworks!

To My Dad

BY SEAN FRASER

Tell me dumb jokes
Take me fishing
Call me when you're gone
Come to my basketball games
Go biking with me
Feed Rocky when I forget
Rock me when I forget

Dad

Become a Poet!

Here are some activities to help you write your own poems.

Keep a Journal

Many writers keep a journal, which is a book of ideas, thoughts, and drawings. Start your own journal in an empty notebook. Write down ideas for your own poems. Write down things that happen, what you like and don't like. Keep your journal with you so you can use it often.

Learn New Words

In the back of your journal, make a list of new words you learn. Start with the words you learned while reading the poems in this book. Write down each word and what it means. Then write each word in a sentence to make sure you know how to use it. Also write down how to say it if you think you won't remember.

Make a Picture

Draw or paint a picture about one of the poems in this book. Maybe pick one of the poems that has many words about colors and other things you can see. Share both the poem and the picture with someone.

Write a Story

Choose one of the poems in this book and write a story from it. Your story can be about what's happening in the poem or who's in the poem. Write using your own words, not the words from the poem.

Have a Poetry Reading

With a few friends or family members, put on a show where everyone has a turn to read a poem out loud. When people aren't reading, they should be in the audience. Practice using correct rhythm and rhyme beforehand. Also make sure you know all the words. Try reciting the poem from memory, if you can.

Find More Poems

What's your favorite poem in this book? Who wrote it? Use the Internet and books in your library to find another poem by this poet. Read the new poem several times. Then read your favorite poem again. How are the two poems alike? How are they different? Which poem do you like best now? Write about the poems in your journal.

Learn About Poets

Use the Internet or books in your library to learn about famous poets. Start with Robert Pottle, who writes a lot of children's poems. Where is he from? What poems has he written? Read four poems by Robert Pottle and pick your favorite. Write down in your journal why you like this poem the best.

Make a Recording

Record yourself reading one of the poems from this book out loud. Practice so you can read the poem with the correct rhythm and rhyme. Ask your parent or teacher for help, if you need it. Record other poems later to make a set of your favorite poems.

Glossary

askew – out of line.

decade – 10 years.

disregard – to pay no attention to.

echo – to repeat the sound.

foreign – of a different country.

ought – should.

proclaim – to announce in public.

regain – to get back or recover.

restore – to make something like it used to be.

soar – to fly high in the sky.

temple – a place of worship.

torment – to cause pain or suffering.

permissions

Index